Mom
To Mom

Other Books by Elisa Morgan

Chronicles of Childhood
I'm Tired of Waiting!
Prayers from a Mother's Heart
What Every Mom Needs (with
Carol Kuykendall)

Audio by Elisa Morgan

A Celebration of Motherhood
Mom to Mom
What Every Mom Needs

To Paige
I know now that you gave all you could.
Thanks, Mother.

Contents

Acknowledgments

Many thanks to all who have had a part in bringing this book to print. Each of you has played a vital role in giving expression to my hidden questions about mothering. Because of you, I am moving from questions to confidence. Thank you!

To Sandy Vander Zicht—for your provision of a format and vehicle to share what I'm learning with other moms.

To Mary McCormick—for your wisdom.

To Rick Christian—for your advocacy.

To the MOPS International Staff, Leadership Team, and Board—for your input and acceptance as I have asked so many mothering questions.

To Eva and Ethan—for your resilience and unconditional love.

And to Evan—for your unquestioning belief that I can mother—and mother well.

Introduction

CONFESSIONS OF A MOTHER "INFERIOR"

Deep in the heart of a mother are whisperings that day after day curl themselves into question marks. But instead of raising her hand to ask her questions boldly, she hangs back, afraid of ridicule, of looking silly, of having such questions in the first place. These unspoken questions have a way of crippling mothers young and old. Because we don't voice our doubts, because we keep our inadequacies buried, we are never freed of them.

Every mother asks questions in her heart. Burdened moms bring them to me in confidential confessions. I've asked many of my own in private ponderings.

This book asks those questions. It speaks the secret doubts that arise in the wee hours of the night and linger, hauntingly, through the morning. It gives words to worries. It asks out loud what we all wish we could ask: the questions deep in the heart of a mother.

And in response to them? Well, you won't necessarily find answers. These are musings and ponderings, biblical principles and lessons learned, all from a mother who is still mothering. I write these stories, not as some kind of expert on mothering. Far from it. I may lead an organization devoted to nurturing mothers, but in my own minutes as a mom I often wrestle with my adequacy to guide my children. When I have shared these stories with moms of all ages in talks around the country, tears have sprung as if some river very near the surface has finally been tapped and allowed to flow.

This book is intentionally developed to encourage you—a few bites at a time. The chapters are short. In fact, they're designed to be devoured in short ten- to fifteen-minute intervals. As a mom, I know it's tough to get more than that amount of time alone to do anything. You might try reading just one question each week, and chewing on the lesson as you go about your duties. At the end of each chapter are "Confidence Builders"—a few questions for your own reflection. You can think them over alone or with a group of other moms who are also gaining the courage to mull over these matters.

Through this book, I pray that you'll find the courage you need to express the questions hidden in the corners of your days, to expose them to the light, and to gain confidence from asking them.

Mom to Mom,
Elisa

Chapter

ONE

How Do I Do This?

With his father's help, my son completed the construction of a pinewood derby car for Tiger Cubs. Late one evening, he came to me requesting that I paint a thunderbolt on the hood of the car. While he offered specifically calibrated instructions at my elbow, I brushed a yellow zigzag over the red base coat.

Why? I'm a mother.

Daily I shuttle back and forth between swim meets and basketball practice. I go to the store to get stencils for a science project display board and to the doctor's to get an X ray for a sprained ankle, which turns out to be broken. Consequently, I become an expert in the art of applying and reapplying an air cast, all the while convincing the patient of the sensational benefits of wearing such a device when one would rather not.

Why? Because I'm a mom.

I send in applications to camp, search for stray socks, and review spelling words each Thursday night. I buy gallons of milk, brush tangles out of matted, chlorine-colored hair, and try to make myself invisible when I have to fold the laundry in the family room and my kids want to be alone with their friends. I monitor scooping out the cat litter box and emptying the dishwasher while resisting the urge to just do it myself, and read *Ramona* bedside.

Why? I'm a mom.

My mothering routine hasn't always been quite so varied. In the early years my responsibilities consisted largely of making sure that my babies were breathing in the middle of the night and sleeping in the middle of the day. They seemed to require no help from me to eat, eat, eat, eat all the time in between.

Throughout the stages of attachment and separation, individuation and identity formation, a certain voice has challenged me from within. I remember it first during the months when we waited to become parents. It continued its insistent whisperings during those initial late-night feedings. On into the toddler years it spoke to me. And even now, on the steps of adolescence, it demands entrance into my days.

Do you know what you're doing? Do you know how to be a mother?

In spite of the pink-and-blue-edged wonder of new parenthood, there is something terrifying about becoming a mother that lasts through all the stages and ages. When a baby is placed in our arms, we imagine that we'll miraculously know just what to do, how to nurture, how to mother. We imagine an instinctive, fitting response to our child.

Such a response did miraculously materialize the instant I saw each of my children. I could hear Eva crying as my husband, Evan, and I approached the door of the adoption agency. We'd waited for four and one-half years for our precious daughter. I was bursting to know her, love her, mother her.

Inside, we found three-week-old Eva on a table. Just a hard, folding table like you'd find in any church banquet hall. She was lying on a thin blanket, arms reaching out, feet kicking slightly, and crying while the caseworker and the foster mom talked, ignoring her need.

My heart twisted within. *Someone pick up that baby! Someone hold her!*

I looked from caseworker to foster mom to my husband, Evan. But the response came from within me. *Well, I'm the mother.* And I marched over, picked up Eva, and bonded on the spot.

Sometimes I do instinctively respond to a moment with a mothering impulse. Like when I hear a loud noise, silence, and then a wail. My feet take me to the side of my child in less than five seconds flat. Did I fly up the stairs?

In those days of struggling to prepare a meal with a toddler and a baby, I never practiced my calisthenics, "Baby on the hip, bottle just so. Toddler down there—don't step on his toe!" No. One late afternoon during the "arsenic" hour of dinner preparation time, while I was juggling and stirring and enduring a leg clamp, the phone rang. I reached for it, stuck the bottle under my chin to hold it and caught my breath in awe as I realized that God had created chins for a purpose!

Yes. An instinctive response within us motivates us maternally. But, to be honest, such a reaction surprises me. I want to be a good mom. But I've always seemed an unlikely candidate.

I grew up in a broken home. My parents were divorced when I was five. My older sister, younger brother, and I were raised by my alcoholic mother, and we saw our father only rarely.

From my mother I learned that creativity was my friend and that if I thought long and hard enough, I could think my way out of any difficulty. I gleaned a love for celebration and surprise through Christmases, birthdays, and friends. I discovered a love for reading and the blissful escape of journeying to other worlds through words. I grew in independence and in self-reliance and only occasionally turned to others for help. I became a survivor. A vigilant, fortressed queen of a kingdom over which I alone ruled.

These are the "upside" lessons of the "upside-down" reality of living with an alcoholic. I am grateful for them because they have been used to carve out the offering of character in my personhood where there might have been only deficits. But I have also come to see the negative aspects of these qualities as they can cut me off from intimacy and hide me in a warped denial of what is truly mature.

From my mother I learned to be strong and to protect myself. In her alcoholic absence, I sheltered my brother. I acquired confidence and leadership. I learned how to live. But I didn't learn how to mother.

It's understandable that in the days preceding the arrival of my daughter, I struggled with inadequacy. And perhaps it makes sense that in the nights that followed her arrival, I wondered if I'd know what to do. And most likely, it is even logical that in the months and years that have passed since my son, Ethan, came on the scene, I would still stumble over the debris of doubts in my path.

Do you know what you're doing? Do you know how to mother?

The same questions came when I first received the call from a MOPS (Mothers of Preschoolers) International board member who wanted me to consider becoming their first president. *President of MOPS?! Ha! You must be deluded! Represent moms across the country—across the world? When I came from a broken home with the secrets behind the doors? I'm so unsure of how to mother in the first place!*

It took three months of prayer and doubled-up therapy sessions for God to convince me that I was just what he wanted. I began to see all the other women just like me who were tackling the job of mothering—some with worse backgrounds. I began to notice in the eyes of others the same uncertainty I felt. As I opened up, others shared their feelings of inadequacy, their need for help. And even those who came from healthy families voiced fears of not doing it right.

In the years of serving as president of MOPS International, I've become convinced that the very deficit I'd experienced was actually the offering God would have me bring to the task.

And I've come to believe that God doesn't make mistakes. I believe that from the womb, he has known me. From the womb, he has known our children. The words of Psalm 139 are true for us and for our children.

> For you created my inmost being; you knit me together in my mother's womb. . . . My frame was not hidden from you when I was made in the secret place. When I was woven together in the depths of the earth, your eyes saw

my unformed body. All the days ordained for me were written in your book before one of them came to be.

(Psalm 139:13, 15–16)

God knows what he's doing. My parents were sovereignly used to make me into who God desires me to be. I believe this now, although the voice still sometimes whispers doubts to me.

I also believe that Evan and I are God's chosen parents for Eva and Ethan. He has sovereignly chosen us for them and them for us, no matter what I was or did or thought in the past.

In 2 Corinthians 12:9, the apostle Paul quotes Jesus' words, *My grace is sufficient for you, for my power is made perfect in weakness.* Human weakness provides the ideal opportunity for the display of divine power. In another New Testament letter Paul admits, *I can do everything through him who gives me strength* (Philippians 4:13).

Do I know what I'm doing? Do you? Sometimes. But not always. And we don't have to. No one expects us to know it all, do it all, or fix it all. God takes our deficits and makes them his offerings to our children and to our world. All we have to do is let him.

CONFIDENCE BUILDERS

1. In what area do you struggle most as a mom? Why is this area such a challenge for you?

2. How can God use your deficits to actually become an offering for your children? How can he turn your weaknesses into your strengths?

3. What is your part in this process?

God takes our deficits
and makes them his
offerings to our children
and our world.

Chapter

TWO

Am I What My Child Really Needs?

Embroidered on a pillow that once lay in my daughter's crib are words from 1 Samuel 1:27–28:

I prayed for this child, and the LORD has granted me what I asked of him. So now I give him to the LORD. For his whole life he will be given over to the LORD.

As a new parent, I can remember tracing my finger along the stitches of that pillow and wondering when I'd first mouth these words for my child, for my children.

The words belonged to a woman named Hannah, who had been childless for years. That's the Bible's sole description of Hannah: She was childless. In a day when a woman's worth was determined by her fertility, Hannah appeared to be worthless. Paired with Fertile Myrtle—Peninnah, her husband's other wife—Hannah faced her inadequacy day in and day out. Peninnah, the mother of many, paraded her children in front of Hannah, gloating over her tribe.

One year, when Hannah and her husband journeyed to the central sanctuary at Shiloh, where many Jews gathered to worship, Hannah begged God for a child in "bitterness of soul." The priest, Eli, told her that God would answer her request. And indeed, God did. After raising and weaning her son, Samuel, Hannah took him to Eli. Fulfilling her promise to God, she offered Samuel back to God.

So now I give him to the LORD. For his whole life he will be given over to the LORD (1:28).

I first met Hannah during the years when my husband, Evan, and I waited for a child through adoption. Because we had known at marriage that we would be unable to bear children naturally and were convinced that we would one day want a family, we began adoption procedures immediately. Four and a half long years later, we finally received Eva, our first child. Ethan came, unexpectedly quickly, two and a half years later through adoption as well.

In bitterness of soul, I had waited, Hannah-like, for children. While I often doubted my adequacy to mother, I was completely secure in my desire. So, when I ran across this Old Testament friend, I took her example into my heart and held it there. Her prayer became a nursery theme, embroidered on a pillow, calligraphied on a plaque.

But I had never really prayed it.

One night when Eva was almost four years old, I put her to bed in haste. I was worn out from the challenge of her incessant needs along with those of her toddler brother. Like any good mother of preschoolers, I prayed with her and kissed her good night. Then, seconds later, she was up, begging for a drink of water, for another book, for a sixteenth kiss, for more of me. But I didn't have any more of me to give.

So, I did what any good mother of preschoolers would do. I gritted my teeth and got through the moment, but not without a bit of impatience and struggle.

Back in my own room, tucked into my covers with the lights out, I cried. *Will I ever be enough as a mother? Will I ruin my children because of the perennial shortage of me?* Hannah's prayer echoed through my mind: *So now I give her to the Lord. For her whole life she will be given over to the Lord.* And for the first time, I mouthed Hannah's words as my own. *Oh, God, please take Eva. I give her over to you. I trust you. But I don't trust me.*

As I lay there in my inadequacy, God's response surprised me. *Okay. I'll take responsibility for Eva. She is my precious child, and I love her more than you ever could. But do you really trust me with her?*

Sure! I responded.

Do you trust me to oversee her schooling?

Yes.

Do you trust me to protect her health?

Of course!

Do you trust me to select her husband—or to care for her if she remains single?

Absolutely!

Well then, do you trust me to select the very best mother for her and for who I want her to become?

Good question. Did I?

With the covers pulled up tight under my chin, I came to grips with the core question of motherhood. *Will I be an adequate mother for my child? For my children? Am I what they need?*

God's response to me, in question form, has become my answer. There is a sovereign dimension to the creation-selection of our children for our families and of ourselves for their mothers. When God gives children to mothers, he gives them with an eye to who they can become for his glory.

We can be the mothers our children need because each of us is divinely chosen to be the mother of each child under our care. That's the truth God speaks to me in the wee hours of the night and in the stark light of day. Between the lines of the prayer embroidered on a pillow that once lay in my baby's room is a truth that has come to rule my mothering.

CONFIDENCE BUILDERS

1. Do you believe that you are the mother your child needs?

2. What are some examples from your everyday life that support this fact?

3. How does this truth change the way you think and feel about yourself as a mother?

Each of us is divinely chosen to be the mother of each child under our care.

Chapter THREE

What Do I Need to Mother Well?

Soft rustlings came from the next room. I glanced at the clock. Yep. Eva was awake. She was a predictable napper, thank goodness, and I'd enjoyed the break of the past hour with her asleep. I pushed my project aside and went to greet her.

She sat up in bed, her toddler-length hair tousled from a busy sleep. Dimples punctuated her chubby cheeks. Her puffy eyes sparkled at the mere sight of me. Twinkling back at her, I reached down with a wake-up hug. She wrestled herself free of sheets and lifted her arms, blankie in tow.

My nose informed me before my hands registered the dampness. She had wet her bed.

Instantly, the peace brought by the previous hour evaporated. Gritting my teeth against the words of criticism I wanted to unleash, I washclothed her bottom and changed her pants. I set her in front of *Sesame Street*, jerked the sheets off the bed, and

27

announced I'd be back in a minute. Once in the privacy of my basement, I crammed the wet, stinky sheets in the washing machine, all
the while tirading to the walls about potty-training.

First there had been the "potty-train in one day" method. That
was actually kind of fun. I'd partitioned off the linoleum floor surfaces of our home, gathered a stash of children's books, mixed a
myriad of juices, and set Eva running diaperless for the entire afternoon so she could "feel" her need to use the potty. We both enjoyed
the serendipity of the day, and at times she was successful in con-
necting "the urge to go" with the potty-chair.

But the next day there were the normal accidents.

Then we resorted to the "gummy bear" reward system. In a grocery store excursion, I encouraged Eva to select her own reward for
keeping her panties dry. When she chose gummy bears, I guided her
hand as she dipped scoop upon scoop from the bulk-food dispenser
into a plastic bag, which she then carried "all by herself" to the
checkout lane. With money I provided, she proudly paid for her
purchase and we left.

The plan was that every time she used the potty successfully,
she'd receive a gummy bear. Those first few days were filled with
nonstop potty-stops. For every drop she created, I doled out a
gummy bear. We stopped in stores, gas stations, restaurants, schools,
and places of employment. She ate lemon, cherry, orange, lime, and
pineapple bears until I feared for the condition of her teeth. Ever
present in my purse was the plastic bag of bears, although at times it
mushed into a mound of critters that had to be pried apart by sticky
fingers. Basically, the plan worked.

But naptime and bedtime proved immune to the reward system. If Eva wasn't awake, she couldn't "feel" her need to potty, nor respond to the enticement of the waiting gummy bear.

I shoved at the balled-up sheets, forcing them down into the washing machine again. I was stripping, washing, and remaking these sheets twice a day now and had been for about two weeks. I'd had it. Grabbing the detergent box, I reached for the scoop to measure out the suds, all the while grumbling, mumbling, and stumbling out feelings.

That's when it happened. It was as if the detergent box took on a life of its own. Whirling and spinning, it flew about the basement, spilling its contents in arcs of momentum. As I watched it fly about me, I noticed it wasn't really moving on its own, but my hand was slinging it, propelling it about. *I* was flinging the box about the room.

While the box flew, it seemed to make a noise. *Wahh Wa Wa Wahhh. Blahhhh Bla Bla Blahhh*. Like the adults in a *Charlie Brown* cartoon, the voice whined and droned, but the words were unintelligible. The voice was familiar. It was mine. My voice was speaking. What was it saying?

How am I supposed to know how to do this? No one has ever taught me this stuff! I'm sick to death of being the one who has to have the answers! I wish I could be the one to ask the questions!

Looking back, I refer to this as my suds-slinging incident. It is a moment in time when I came to grips with my mothering inadequacies. It stands as a monument in my days, reminding me of how I began to see what I don't have, what I can't do as a mother.

How did the day continue? I don't remember. I know that I somehow composed myself and trudged back up the basement steps to Eva's room, dealt with the accident, cuddled her, and went about the day. I also know that she is, indeed, potty-trained today, some ten years later, and that it didn't take ten years to accomplish this feat. That's not the monument part.

The monument stands in the months that followed when I gradually began to see myself as a needy person, whereas I had never before embraced this aspect of myself. Before, I'd cheerfully assumed that I could handle whatever situation I faced. I always had. I mean, in my growing-up years I'd somehow made it through each day, even those pierced with the unpredictable outbursts of an alcoholic mother.

This moment in the basement brought me face-to-face with some deeper crevice in my being. A gap. A hole. A wound, perhaps. It was empty where it should have been filled.

And as unsettling as it was to experience that emptiness, I now know that it was good for me. I don't know how to do most of what I do with my children. Sure, I can read books and listen to the experts and talk to those who've already been through the spots where I am. But in the everyday moments, it's I who have to make the decisions and come up with the answers. As I search through my mental files for help, more times than not my fingers touch on the questions, not the answers.

In Matthew 5:3, Jesus spoke to the crowd assembled on the mountainside by the Sea of Galilee. With these words, he began what has become the most famous sermon of all time: *Blessed are the poor in spirit, for theirs is the kingdom of heaven.*

Why did he choose these words? Because until we understand our neediness, we can't experience fulfillment. Until we look boldly at our emptiness, we can't be filled. As long as we think we can handle it all, we will. Unless we grasp what we can't do, we won't have a clue to what God can do.

I know now that most moms grit their teeth and smother screams throughout potty-training. I also know that this rite of passage is a normal trial-and-error, success-and-failure reality of development. Eva's process through this period was normal. So was mine. I had a need. And my need was normal.

This suds-slinging incident has changed my life. It has pushed me to begin a journey toward wholeness along an entirely different path. Our inadequacies reveal our needs. And when we experience our needs and then bring them to God, he can meet them. And when he meets them, we can be whole.

CONFIDENCE BUILDERS

1. How do you interpret your neediness as a person? As normal or abnormal?

2. Think back through your days. When have you experienced a "monument" of your neediness? How did you handle it?

3. What do you think Jesus meant when he said, *"Blessed are the poor in spirit for theirs is the kingdom of God"*? Do you see yourself as poor in spirit?

As long as we think we can handle it all, we will. Unless we grasp what we can't do, we won't have a clue to what God can do.

Chapter

FOUR

How Do I Make Good Choices?

I pulled up to the crosswalk and waved to my children. Shifting backpacks, they opened car doors and slid into seats. As we covered the few blocks between school and home, they unleashed tales of their days. We pulled into the garage to find Evan's car in the next slot.

"Daddy's home!" Eva and Ethan erupted simultaneously. Even after a decade of mothering and fathering together, I was still amazed at their response to their father, simply because he is their father. He seemed to entertain them and hold a cherished spot in their hearts like some giant, treasured toy, regardless of their years. Mom, on the other hand, was a mere necessity. They noticed me most when there wasn't any food in the refrigerator, or I couldn't drive them to a friend's house.

I smiled. I, too, was glad that Evan was home.

After the routine of dropping backpacks and jackets inside the door, kicking off shoes, and then retracing steps to pick up backpacks, jackets, and shoes, I made my way to the family room, where Evan lay on the couch, the back of his forearm resting over his eyes. He was sick. Now I wasn't so glad to see him. Instead of the hope of help, I faced the added presence of yet another need in my already packed afternoon.

I sighed and directed the children to the kitchen table for homework. After that came dinner. I dug microwave meals out of the freezer. Then the cleanup. By now Evan was upstairs in bed, the kids were sprawled out in front of the TV, and I, still in hose and heels, was slapping peanut butter and jelly on bread for tomorrow's lunches. Left on my list for the night were two loads of laundry left from yesterday and preparations for a speaking engagement I had to leave for the next morning.

At seven o'clock, I pointed the kids toward the stairs, and their stacks of socks, shoes, books, waiting to be carried up to their rooms. Ah, almost there. Just baths and prayers and then I could get back to the wash and the talk I had to complete.

I picked up my own pile of mail and laundry and mounted the stairs, but as I reached the landing, my eyes fell on an unsightly mound of orange-green-gray something. The cat had thrown up. And by the sight of the lump of stuff, the offense had occurred some time earlier that day. Children, husband, and who-knows-who had been up and down the stairs umpteen times that day, gingerly stepping past and not on the pile.

I lost it. I threw down my stack of stuff and harrumphed, "Well, what is this delightful mess on the stairs?!" At the top of my lungs I continued, "How thoughtful of you all to save this special surprise for me to find!"

I stomped down the stairs to the kitchen to grab paper towels. Pulling on the end of the roll, I tugged, whereupon about forty towels whipped out across the counter. Ripping off an armload, I returned, stomping the entire way, to the stair landing.

"Is the mother the only person in the house who knows how to clean up cat vomit?!" I queried. *Sop. Sop. Sop.* I sponged towel after towel on the stinking mess.

"Is the mother the only person in the house who knows where the paper towels are?!" *Squish. Squish. Squish.* I wrinkled my nose as the towels oozed their contents.

"Is the mother the only one in this house who knows where to take stinky paper towels when they are full of cat vomit?!" *Thunk. Thunk. Thunk.* I marched to the garage and slammed the door behind me.

I raised the garbage can lid, deposited the grungy gunk, and banged the lid down. That sounded good. We have metal garbage cans. The good old-fashioned galvanized steel kind. Not rose or stone-blue Rubbermaid. Ours are shiny steel. The lid makes lots of noise when it hits the can. It sounded great! No, it sounded *wonderful!*

Clang! Bang! Crash! Wham! Once again. *Clang! Bang! Crash! Wham!* Ah... Now I was getting somewhere. *Clang! Bang! Crash! Wham!*

I raised my arm for one more good *Bang!* when I seemed to hear inside, *Elisa.* I stopped to listen. *Elisa.* I knew who it was.

Elisa, you have a speaking engagement in the morning, right? You have only about fifteen minutes left to get through tonight. Your husband

is sick. Your kids need you. Now, you have a choice. You can either con-
tinue this fit, or you can get a grip and go handle things. Then you can
take a break. What are you going to do?

Hmmm. Now this was a real choice. What I wanted to do was get in the car and drive far, far away. I didn't want to go back in the house and deal with cat vomit, unbathed children, a sick husband, two loads of wash, or preparations for a speaking engagement. What was I speaking on, anyway? Oh, yeah. Matthew 6:33: *But seek first his kingdom and his righteousness, and all these things will be given to you as well.*

With the trash can lid still poised in my hand, I thought through what I had studied about the passage. We are to seek God. Actually, the phrase Jesus used directs us to hunt for God continuously, as if we were hunting for food. We're not to look for God just when we feel like it or when it's convenient. We're to hunt for him in each moment of life as if we desperately need him just to survive the day or the night. When we seek him, in a relationship of daily or nightly dependence, he'll give us whatever else we need, because most of all, what we need is him.

I lowered the lid and trudged back inside. I reclimbed the stairs, picked up my pile, and turned to face my staring children. "Guys, Mom's wasted. I just lost it, and I'm sorry. Could you please give me a hand? Let's make this next few minutes run smoothly together—okay?"

Biting back the laughter, they agreed and headed off to brush their teeth.

My toughest choices as a mom haven't centered on whether or not to work outside the home, or whether or not to send my children to public school or Christian school, or even whether or not to home school them. While these have been difficult decisions, my most challenging choices continue to come when I stand with myself and determine how I will live out each moment I face. Will I be the woman I want to be? And if so, will I take the steps necessary to make that happen?

God never asked us to meet all by ourselves every need we face. There simply isn't enough of us to do so. But God is enough. And in his enough, we're enough. And for me, that's good enough.

CONFIDENCE BUILDERS

1. As a mom, what choices have you faced lately? Which ones have been the most difficult and why?

2. What do you do when you run out of "you"?

3. How could "seeking" God help you choose well?

Our most challenging choices come as we stand with ourselves and determine how we will live out each moment we face. No, there's not enough of us. But when there's not enough of us, there's always more of God. And in his enough, we're enough.

How Do I Handle My Imperfections?

Before I tell you this story, I need to assure you that I love cats. I always have. When I was eight, I begged my mother, who was a dog lover, for a cat. She ignored my pleas, stalled my overtures, and then finally gave in. In the years that followed, I have self-sacrificially cared for my cats as I would have cared for my own children. I rescued one from the top of a forty-foot poplar tree. I gave shots to another who was diagnosed with a fatal disease, and I actually nursed her back to health. In the middle of the night I've endured kneading paws in the nape of my neck. While immersed in a novel, I've made room on my lap to accommodate an incessant need for cuddling. I've willingly succumbed to my own children when they've pleaded for a cat—one each—and have taken it upon myself to litter-box train and care for these new additions to our family in the years when my children were too young to care for them independently. And though sometimes I've been miffed, I've obediently cleaned up fur balls and other messes left behind by my cats. So, as you read the following, remember this: I really do love cats.

One winter morning, I was shoveling snow off the driveway, minding my own business. My neighbor pulled her car up to the curb, rolled down her window, and presented her Christmas-gift-of-the-year idea to me. "How about," she suggested, "if we help our daughters make matching sweatshirts for each other to exchange at the neighborhood children's party? We won't tell them that they, too, are receiving one, only that they're making one. They'll be so surprised when they tear open their gifts to find them matching!"

Quickly, heartily, enthusiastically, I agreed. Moments later, watching her car's exhaust trail up the street, I realized that I had no clue about how to make a sweatshirt myself, much less assist Eva in the process. A panic-filled phone call to my neighbor later that afternoon left me armed with a list of necessary purchases from the fabric store and detailed instructions. I was to buy a large white sweatshirt, the Daisy Kingdom Bunny appliqué, and a specific selection of pink, blue, green, and black fabric paint.

Like most Decembers, this particular December was frantic with chores that promised to make Christmas magical but in reality only created a grumpy mom. On Saturday morning, hours before the children's Christmas party, Eva and I descended the stairs to our basement, with paraphernalia in hand and anticipation in heart. Choosing the only flat, clean surface in our basement on which to work, we carefully laid out the sweatshirt, appliqué, and paints atop the washer and dryer.

The sweat beaded up on my brow as my nervous fingers peeled back the appliqué and I pressed the iron down on the shirt. At my elbow, Eva giggled with excitement. *Ah . . . Isn't this great?* Mother-daughter bonding time. Bonding, bonding, bonding, are we bonding? I checked the appliqué. Yes, we were bonding.

Next came the green paint around the grass. Then the black paint. *Oh, this is a challenge.* "I'll do that, Eva," I said. Black paint on a white sweatshirt, around the edges of the Daisy Kingdom bunnies, up around the ears. *Hey! We can do this!* All done, we bounded up the stairs to attend to other tasks.

Two hours later I decided I'd better check on the sweatshirt. *Is it dry yet? It's so good to have that checked off my list today!* I trundled down the stairs and approached the washer and dryer.

Something looked askew.

I looked more closely at the washer and dryer. The sweatshirt was tilted at a bizarre angle on the lid of the washer, its long arm dangling precariously off the edge.

I was concerned.

On my tiptoes, more gingerly now, I moved forward, afraid of what I might discover. Another step. Black spots covered the lid of my white washing machine. Inky smudges trailed across the sweatshirt, over the washing machine, down its side, and over the floor where they weren't before and where they shouldn't ever be.

I bent to inspect these spots. I did not need a magnifying glass. I could tell at a glance that these were no ordinary black spots. They had the size and shape of a paw print. Measuring the circumference of the paw print, I ascertained that it was the print of the large, white cat—the one that *used to* belong to Eva.

Here's where it gets a little sticky, this story. The sweatshirt had to be wrapped by four o'clock for the neighborhood Christmas party. It was now 2:00. There was no time to re-create a replacement and get it dry and wrapped. We *had* to go to this party. I couldn't let my neighbor or her daughter down! What would they think? We were the ones who knew Jesus. Most of the rest of the neighborhood didn't.

But instead of problem-solving a present at the moment, I prowled around on my hands and knees in search of a white cat that used to be welcome in our house. I made my way through dust balls, stacks of boxes, and set-aside holiday decorations until I found him cowering under a party piñata.

He looked at me and I looked at him. I was bigger, but he was faster. I lunged. He sprang. I caught him. All kinds of options ran through my head. Hitting, kicking, throwing. *No, I can't do that. That would hurt him. No, no, no. No matter how much a mess he's made, I mustn't hurt this cat.*

So, I bit the cat. Right on the top of his head in the furry part below his ear. I didn't bite him hard. I promise. It was just a nibble.

Remember, I really do love cats.

Staring at my cat and then at the paw-printed sweatshirt, I knew I was doomed. The black blotches across the white surfaces mirrored my own imperfections. There was no way I could complete my end of the deal with my neighbor. Her daughter would be disappointed when there was no box for her to open. No matching sweatshirt surprise. No perfect present.

In 2 Corinthians 13:11 we read, *Aim for perfection* . . . Colossians 1:28 relates Paul's goal of presenting everyone mature and complete in Christ. In Matthew 5:48, Jesus himself said, *Be perfect, therefore, as your heavenly Father is perfect.* In these verses, God gives us his goal for us. One day, he hopes I'll look just like him.

But right now? Am I supposed to be perfect today? I don't think so. Becoming like Jesus is a process. God forgives us our sins when we come into a relationship with Jesus as Savior and Lord. Then he begins the process of making us like him in the day-to-day moments of life. God knows that we won't be perfect today. Complete perfection is reserved for a time in the future. Today is the time we are supposed to be imperfect, cat-nibbling, dependent humans, in need of a Savior. We're not done yet. If we were done, we'd be dead.

We can't be perfect today. But we can make it a daily practice to walk in the direction of perfection, seeing at the end of our journey the goal of becoming like Christ.

I got in my car, drove to the fabric store, and bought another large white sweatshirt and Daisy Kingdom Bunny appliqué. I wrapped them up in a box with a note that promised the finished product as soon as the paint could dry. Later, at the party, my neighbor beamed. Her daughter hugged mine while my daughter gasped with delight over the matching sweatshirt she received. I went home glad for what I'd learned. And still picking the fur from my teeth.

CONFIDENCE BUILDERS

1. How do you handle your imperfections?

2. What does it mean to "walk in the direction of perfection"? How can you do that?

God knows we won't be perfect today. Complete perfection is reserved for a time in the future. We're not done yet. If we were done, we'd be dead.

Chapter

SIX

How Does God See
Me When I Fail?

I t was late in the morning one dreary December day. I'd carefully
timed the trip to the gift-shop-turned-UPS store to correspond
with my nine-month-old's nap, so I could keep her buckled in her
carseat and under control. Going out in public had become risky
business since she'd taken up walking ahead of schedule.

It had been snowing, and maneuvering along the icy streets was
no easy task. I searched out a spot semi-close to the door. Lately, I'd
battled images of my slipping and careening across the sidewalk
with my daughter flying out of my arms through the air. With extra
care, I hauled her out in her carseat and balanced atop her bunting
the first of eight Christmas packages to be mailed. Hoisting my load
on my hip, I grabbed the store's door handle and in one motion,
threw the door back while cramming my free hip, leg, and foot into
the opening. I proceeded to the counter, where I dumped the package and then returned to my car, carseat and baby on hip. I

performed this process seven times. (One of my packages was small, so I risked a double-decker trip.)

By the time my parcels were stacked three-deep on the makeshift counter, sweat was streaming down my back beneath my turtleneck sweater and parka.

"Whew!" I announced to the clerk awaiting my orders. I admit it, it was an attempt to elicit some expression of empathy. After all, she had stood watching the whole proceeding with great interest but little involvement.

"I'm exhausted!" I panted, looking up for even a glimpse of shared pain.

The response I received still sticks in my memory. "I'm sorry, but we can't accept parcels with string. The new code specifically directs the use of package tape only. You'll have to rewrap these if you want them mailed."

And there, in the gift-shop-turned-UPS-headquarters, I, Elisa Morgan, became unglued.

"What?" I squeaked. "I don't have any packaging tape!" Despite my best effort to arm-wrestle my tongue to the floor of my mouth, out popped, "How could you watch me slop back and forth between my car and the counter, baby in tow, and never stop me or say anything?!"

"Here are some scissors. Would you like to purchase some packing tape?" came the monotone reply.

"Oh, yes, I'll borrow your scissors." *Snip. Snip. Snip.* "And I'll take a roll of that tape marked up five times more than they charge at the grocery store." *Rip. Rip. Rip.*

I wrote out my check and thrust it at her, along with my ID.

"Elisa Morgan," she murmured. "Didn't you speak at a retreat for my church recently?"

I wanted to shrink down to the size of a slug and slither my way back out the door, all without her noticing. I sincerely think I would have at least tried, except for the ice on the pavement outside the door. I hate ice.

"You never know who's watching, do you?" she queried.

"Nope. You don't," I responded, fully rebuked.

> Nothing in all creation is hidden from God's sight. Everything is uncovered and laid bare before the eyes of him to whom we must give account.
>
> (Hebrews 4:13)

I picked up my now-awake baby and heaved her up before me. From her cuddled-in spot, still strapped in her carseat, she beamed at me. She didn't seem to notice my red-faced shame. To her I was still Mom—perfect because I was there. I was hers.

But who was I to others? To the world around me? To God? *No, nothing is hidden. Everything is revealed. Everything.*

God saw my good intentions of mailing efficiently while balancing a baby and other demands. He saw my struggle to get the packages to the counter while caring for my child. And he saw me, in exasperation, slip.

Nothing is hidden. Everything is revealed.

The marvelous truth is that God doesn't just reveal. He doesn't simply stack up sins on one side and good deeds on the other and then back up to measure with a squint. No, he reveals and then covers.

But God demonstrates his own love for us in this: While we were still sinners, Christ died for us.

(Romans 5:8)

In Greek this verse conveys the message that while we were *in the process of sinning*, Jesus died once for all our sins. Ah. While I was in the process of struggling to manage baby and responsibilities. While I was in the process of managing, or mismanaging, my temper. And even now, while I'm in the process of evaluating my failure.

No, we never know who's watching. But we do know who's always revealing and covering, seeing and forgiving.

CONFIDENCE BUILDERS

1. How do you respond when you make a mistake? What do you say in your mind? How do you evaluate yourself?

2. How do you imagine God sees you when you fail? Try to picture him looking at you and then seeing yourself from his perspective.

3. How does understanding God's view of your failure change your response to yourself when you fail?

Thankfully, the God who sees us in our worst moments does not measure us by them.

Chapter

SEVEN

Do I Notice When
I Do It Right?

Ethan and I pushed the grocery cart down the cereal aisle, searching for a compromise between sugar and fiber. He was in a happy mood, clicking his well-loved cowboy boots on the shiny linoleum as we passed the Frosted Flakes. Up ahead, we both spotted another couple approaching us—a mom and her son. He was about seven, about the same age as Ethan.

Then it happened, catching both of us by surprise. Ethan's feet flew out from under him, and he landed splat on his face between the Cheerios and the Grape Nuts. The combination of his slick boots and the highly polished floor must have been the culprit.

The little boy and his mom giggled and tried to pass while Ethan struggled in a heap. From his contorted position on the floor, Ethan evaluated his options. After a second, he smiled gleefully and announced, "That was fun! That's just what I meant to do!"

57

I looked down at him and then up the aisle at the mom and child now glancing back over their shoulders. Matching Ethan's enthusiasm, I said, "Yep. It's even better than last time. I bet, on the next aisle you'll do it even better!" I tugged him upright and together we wheeled around the corner, leaving our observers staring after us.

As soon as we were out of earshot, Ethan, still holding my hand, beamed up at me. "Thanks for sticking up for me, Mom!"

I ruffled his hair, laughed, and continued my grocery hunt. But my mind lingered on the event. *Why had I taken Ethan's side?* On so many other occasions that wouldn't have been my natural response. Instead of sticking up for Ethan, I would have said, "Quit goofing around—you'll hurt yourself!" or "See what happens when you're showing off?"

But not this time. On this occasion, out of me came a clever contrivance that said we were in on a scheme together, and my response built a rock-solid base of security beneath his could-have-been humiliated self. It was one of those moments when Jesus grabbed hold of me and wrestled his words out of my mouth.

I hadn't planned it. If I'd thought hard about it, I'm not sure I would have said what I said. And without thinking, a more likely response would have been, "Way to go—klutz!" But in the moment, the words came, the response was automatic. God seemed to intervene and match my offering to Ethan's need. He also matched Ethan's need to my offering.

The only miracle that all four gospel writers record—besides the Resurrection—is the feeding of the five thousand. When something like that happens in the Bible, I figure there must be a reason. If a truth is worth telling four times, it must be worth hearing in the heart.

Jesus had taught a huge crowd and, as the day deepened to dusk, his disciples came to him, concerned that the people were hungry and should be sent to neighboring cities to eat. Jesus' response? He told the disciples to feed them.

Five thousand people? "That would take eight months of a man's wages!" one disciple roared at the absurdity of such a thought.

How did Jesus respond? Mark tells us that Jesus asked, "How many loaves do you have? Go and see." They trotted off to find out. When they had counted, they reported the handful to Jesus. So with a few loaves and fish, Jesus directed them to feed some five thousand people. The story ends with the report that many baskets full of broken pieces of bread and fish were left over after all had eaten and were satisfied.

Most of the time, we don't have any idea how many loaves we have. We saunter down the cereal aisle, expecting to pick up a box of Wheaties to feed our families, and God offers us the chance to feed the souls of our children.

With what? we wonder.

What do you have? Jesus responds. And he takes our offering and matches it to the need of our child.

I smiled and turned down the cookie aisle, Ethan tromping happily at my side. Hmmm. Not long ago I'd wondered if I could do anything right as a mother. Today I waltzed through the unexpected, not just unscathed but triumphant. Enough analysis. I decided to savor the moment. With a gleam in my eye I reached for the Pepperidge Farm Mint Milanos. Ethan's eyes widened. Yes, this was definitely something to celebrate.

CONFIDENCE BUILDERS

1. Think back over the past week or so. What did you do right?

2. How does it bring you confidence in your mothering to keep a tally of your successes?

3. How many "loaves" do you have today? Plan to be on the watch today for ways in which you surprise even yourself with how God uses your resources to meet the needs of your child.

God matches our
offering to the need of
our child and the need of
our child to our offering.

EIGHT

How Do I Teach My Child to Live Life Well?

Ethan whirled through the front door and slammed it behind him. Stomping upstairs, he raced to his room and banged the door shut. I followed and knocked gently.

"What!" came the response.

Twenty minutes later, after a heart-to-heart wrestling of information out of my eight-year-old son, I learned that Rob, up the street, had excluded Ethan from a game of street hockey, and Ethan hadn't handled it well. He was steamed. With his face twisted up in angry lines, Ethan denied any responsibility for his part in the exchange. No matter that he, too, had lost his temper or called his friend a name.

These are challenging moments for moms. One dimension of me wanted to rise to Ethan's defense. I considered calling Rob's mom and insisting that Rob include my brilliantly talented son in his precious little game.

But the more saintly aspect of my soul opted to use this struggle to help Ethan learn something about himself, about his temper, and about relationships. So I worked with him on the difference between appropriately and inappropriately expressed anger, on taking responsibility for his own errors, and even on apologizing for his part in the problem. Five more minutes were given to explaining the benefits of apologies, how they build bridges instead of barriers, how when we assume appropriate responsibility, we encourage others to do the same. You know the lines.

Eventually Ethan agreed with the logic and phoned Rob, mumbling a few words into the mouthpiece and listening while Rob did the same. Progress.

The next morning, in the space of just a few minutes, Eva revealed that she hadn't finished her homework; Ethan had dawdled extra-long over his hair-combing process; and I realized that I was supposed to be working in Ethan's class that morning and had scheduled something else during that time slot. I felt an edginess within me spring to the surface.

When Ethan finally made it to breakfast, he was in a rotten mood. Vestiges from yesterday's bout hung about him like a shroud. He grunted responses to my offers of breakfast choices. He rolled his eyes at my warnings. He outright disobeyed my final command to get his attitude straight.

I'd been patient. I'd empathized with his hurt feelings. I'd preached truth and righteousness and had even supervised retribution. *I'd fixed him, hadn't I? What was wrong with him now? Why didn't he move past this spot?*

Breakfast dishes were spread across the counter. *Why can't these kids learn to rinse their stuff and put it in the dishwasher? Why is it always my responsibility?* I grabbed plates and bowls and glasses, stuck them under the faucet and onto the drain board. I threw back the dishwasher door, letting it bounce up and down from the momentum. I snatched the top rack and jerked it out. Three at a time, I stuffed juice glasses in their wire partitions.

A door slammed upstairs. Turning, I noticed that Ethan had left the table without eating a bite. The clock showed 8:25. Five minutes to the first school bell. And we were still here, in a mess.

"Ethan!" I hollered up the stairs. "Come down here right now!" Then the tears came. Mine, not Ethan's. It was too much. When would he learn to handle his anger in a healthy manner?

I'd left the door to the dishwasher down while calling up to Ethan, and when I came back around the kitchen counter, my shin banged against its corner. *Aahhh!* Pain ricocheted up my leg. With whirlwind force, I threw the door up, clanging it against the still-extended upper rack, and shoving rack, glasses, and cups back into their hole in one singular motion. The catch caught with a click, and I heard a slight tinkling sound from within.

By now I was ranting to myself. I do my best soul-searching in such moments. I guess it's because I'm finally listening to what I've been trying to say all along. *Well, isn't this grand? Here I am trying to teach Ethan how to handle his anger, and look at me. What kind of model am I?*

With great care, I opened the dishwasher door. More tinkling sounds. I apprehensively peered inside. It was not a pretty sight. Shards from what used to be three juice glasses hung at odd angles from the upper rack. Fragments of glass lay, tilted, over the dishes on the bottom rack. I lifted one cup—it was chipped but still intact.

> Woe to you, teachers of the law and Pharisees, you hypocrites! You clean the outside of the cup and dish, but inside they are full of greed and self-indulgence. Blind Pharisee! First clean the inside of the cup and dish, and then the outside also will be clean.

> (Matthew 23:25–26)

I guess it was the cup that reminded me of Jesus' words to the Pharisees. Sick to death of the Pharisees' hypocrisy, Jesus judged them as fools. They were more concerned about external appearances than internal truth, and they busied themselves with teaching others to focus on the nonessentials rather than on what really mattered. The core of their teaching ran something like this: "Don't worry about the inside of you as a person; just make sure you look good on the outside."

Was I so different? Here I was, trying so hard to make the outside of the cup clean that I'd forgotten all about the inside. I'd been so concerned that Ethan "fix" things with Rob that I hadn't allowed him the opportunity for his heart to get right first. What had leaked out this morning over breakfast was his still-present need. He wasn't ready. And that was okay.

And I? I was so concerned that I "fix" Ethan that I hadn't given my own heart the chance to process what I needed to. When Ethan didn't respond precisely as I thought he should, I felt like a failure as a mom. With each step he took away from my goal, I tightened my grip of insistence that he do it "my way." Inside my cup was stubbornness and a senseless need to be right. It's not my job to "fix" my children. That responsibility belongs to God. My job is to be in an honest and truthful place with God myself and to live that way before my children. In my efforts to manage Ethan's temper, I'd lost my own. Granted, it wasn't a fit of rage as much as it was a response to the pain in my shin and the frustration of the moment. But in my desire to clean the outside of my cup, I'd overlooked the attention needed by the inside.

The tears flowed easily now. I was broken, and I didn't need to pretend otherwise. I turned from the debris to the clock. But before I could register the time, Ethan was there before me, with tears of his own and arms flung about my waist. I bent to embrace him, apologizing for my outburst, for my impatience with him, for my zealous insistence that he be "fixed."

My precious son looked up at me with beaming love and replied, "That's okay, Mom. We all make mistakes. I'm sorry too."

Later that day I thought back over this bizarre ending to our twenty-four-hour ordeal and mused that maybe I wasn't such a bad model after all. Yes, Ethan had seen me blow it in an area where he, himself, needed to learn control, but he'd also observed me making things right again. He'd watched me fail, and he'd been the recipient of my apology. We teach our children to live life well by modeling life-living before them, including our triumphs, failures, and apologies. What more could a child ask for in a laboratory experience of how to live life?

CONFIDENCE BUILDERS

1. When you think about teaching your child how to live life
    well, what methods come quickly to mind? Of the options
    you've considered, which have been the most effective in
    your experience?

2. How do you feel about your child's learning from your
    example?

3. Are there danger spots to avoid in expecting your children
    to learn from your example? What are they, and how can
    you be on guard for them?

It's not our job to "fix" our children. That responsibility belongs to God.

Chapter

NINE

What If I Don't Know the Answers?

"Can I use the scissors?"

"Do I have to make my bed?"

"When are you going to work in my classroom?"

All of these questions came to me within the period of one hour. In seconds, I was expected to provide answers. Mature, mother answers. Right and wise answers. Another call for "Answer Mom."

"Answer Whom"? How do I know whether or not to insist on bed making this instant? If I ease up, will I reinforce laziness? If I make a major issue of it, will I curtail her independence? Speaking of independence, should a preschooler truly handle a pair of scissors? And oh, what does it mean when my child wants me to work in his classroom? Is he feeling insecure or unsure? Should I reschedule my plans to be there this week instead of my previously assigned time next month?

I've often thought that it would be the questions of childhood that would bring about my demise. But now I realize it's not their questioning. It's my answering—the pressure to pontificate with age-appropriate wisdom to meet the unseen need beneath the question.

Ha! How do I know the answers when most of the time I barely understand the questions? "Answer Mom"! Where are you?

Lately, it seems as if I call out for "Answer Mom" while schlepping my kids about in the car. I don't want you to get the wrong impression. Our discussions aren't always spiritual. To be honest, most of our car conversations center on who gets to sit in the front on the way home from the store, or why we can't stop at Dairy Queen a half hour before dinner. But one particular evening on the way to swim practice, we quizzed each other on the miracles in the Bible.

"Jonah in the whale!" Ethan yelled. "Turning water into wine!" hollered Eva. This continued until we'd covered everything from Daniel in the lions' den to Jesus' walking on water.

Putting on my best Sunday school teacher voice, I asked, "Which miracle do you think is the most amazing of all?"

Silence.

I filled in the blank. "I think the most amazing miracle is that God raised Jesus from the dead."

"Yeah," they agreed.

We got out of the car, Eva towing her swim satchel over her shoulder. Walking up the steps to the pool, she asked, "Mom, when you become a Christian, is it kind of like you die on the cross with Jesus?"

"Uh . . . well, no . . . not exactly. But then again, sorta . . . uh . . .," I stammered.

Oh, great, another call for "Answer Mom"! What was I supposed to say? What was the right answer?

In Isaiah 40:11, God speaks a radically comforting sentence: *He tends his flock like a shepherd: He gathers the lambs in his arms and carries them close to his heart; he gently leads those that have young.*

This verse is a part of a chapter that focuses on God's calling his people out of captivity in Babylon and home to himself, out of a life separated from him and into a relationship of stability and security, close to his heart. God uses the analogy of shepherd and sheep to express his tender concern for his people. Close to his heart, they can draw on the guidance and compassion he daily supplies.

And so can we. Bending low, he swoops us into his arms, carrying our successes and failures as well. Cradling us close to his heart, in his bosom, on his very lap, he welcomes our cries for help and gently leads those who have young.

He carries. He cradles. He guides. He holds us with our young in his arms.

When it's ten at night, we've been up since five, and we face three more loads of wash and a set of bottles to prepare, we need to be carried. When we climb the stairs during what we thought was naptime to discover that our eighteen-month-old has baptized his crib with his messy diaper, we need to be cradled. When we're racing from a trip to the store (to buy chocolate chips to make cookies for the bake sale we forgot is tomorrow) to swim practice—and our child asks a question we barely comprehend—we need a friend.

The friend is found in Jesus—and in the conversations we have with him in his Word. When we spend time reading the Bible, we discover that God never asks us to be "Answer Mom." In his "Answer Book" we find he has something to say about how we can live in a relationship close to his heart day in and day out and that from that posture we'll acquire the wisdom to cope with the questions our children bring.

He may not speak to whether or not five-year-olds should use scissors, but he lets us know that he trusts us to handle such a decision with wisdom, because he's in the thick of life with us. He helps us figure out whether, in this moment, a bed must be made. And next week, he'll be there when we believe it's best to reverse the decision of today.

Close to his heart. That's where he says he'll put us, we who have young. I don't know about you, but I can't think of a better place to be.

CONFIDENCE BUILDERS

1. What strategies have you developed to deal with the incessant questions of your children?

2. What does it mean to you to live "close to God's heart"?

3. Can you imagine God's carrying you like a lamb? What would that be like? In what situation today do you need God to carry you?

God never asks us to be "Answer Moms." In his "Answer Book" we find he has something to say about how we can live close to his heart day in and day out, and from that posture we'll acquire the wisdom we need to cope with the questions our children bring. "Close to his heart"—that's where God says he'll put us, we who have young ones. I don't know about you, but I can't think of a better place to be.

Chapter

TEN

When Is It Okay to Ask for Help?

Evan had left for work that morning about an hour before it started: a queasy rumbling from somewhere deep within my stomach. I dressed Eva for preschool, gathered baby Ethan on my hip, and clumped downstairs to prepare breakfast.

Good thing Eva's favorite breakfast is Cheerios, I consoled myself. By now my head was swimming, and I'd made several dashes for the bathroom. With my chin propped on my palms and my elbows stuck to the breakfast table, I gazed at my children. Eva slurped spoonful after soggy spoonful of cereal into her eager mouth, her eyes glued to Blinky's Fun Club on the TV. Ethan, still in his sunny yellow footie jammies, chased dry Cheerios around his high chair tray. His downy hair stood straight up from his scalp in a just-woke-up early-morning tousle. Mine probably didn't look much better.

"Oh no!" An urge erupted from within me, and I lurched for the bathroom again. There surely wasn't much left in me to come out!

When I returned, it was clear that no one had missed me. Eva had moved on to her juice, sucking from the Tupperware Tippy lid. Ethan was staring out the window, his tray now empty, and the floor beneath him dotted with clever, escape-artist O's.

While they'd made it this far without me, I knew they wouldn't last. Any moment now, they'd moan, or question, or simply walk near me. I had to make a plan. I commanded my arm to reach for the phone. It obeyed. Amazing. Then I told my fingers to dial. They did. A voice came on the other end.

"Mmrpheedy," it said.

"Eeevvvvaannnnnnnmuyrp Morgggggapgh, phhhleeezzzphr," I responded.

"Whoorrppry?" the voice asked.

I realized that my head was lying across the phone, sandwiching it between my ear and the table. No wonder I couldn't understand the voice. I straightened my torso, raised the phone a few inches, and tried again.

"Evaaannn Morrgggan, pllleeeze." Ah. There was a pause and then my dear husband's secretary, LuAnne, came on the line. Terrific! Except that by now the bathroom beckoned me again, and I was forced to leave the phone and LuAnne's comforting presence. Bless her heart, she was still there when I returned. But my exhilaration in her patience evaporated when she reported that Evan was out the office and wouldn't be back for several hours.

No help there. I punched the phone off and focused on the clock. I had no other choice. Preschool started in twenty minutes. And with the flu, one child was much easier to handle than two. I had to get Eva there. And I had to get me and Ethan back. Or I would die. I was sure of it.

"OOOOOOhhhhhh Nooooooohhhhh..." and I was gone again.

You know how there is that wonderful afterglow that follows a flu-bathroom call? For a few minutes—sometimes as many as fifteen, you feel whole and healthy and like, *Hey, I'm going to be okay after all!* You know? Well, it was during such a moment that I buckled both Eva and Ethan into their carseats, grabbed my keys, and headed out.

An inner compulsion directed me back to the house for something round and sturdy and deep, just in case. My Dutch oven was too heavy. The mixing bowl might break. I eyed Eva's Tippy cup. No way. Ah... the butter tub. It was jumbo-sized, and I'd just rinsed it out. Perfect.

Ten minutes later, somewhere between the house and preschool, I drove with one hand while balancing the butter tub beneath my chin with the other. Finally, I pulled into the parking lot, left Ethan strapped in, and allowed Eva to run through the doors ahead of me. I'd made it. But the satisfaction of my accomplishment was short-lived. I dashed down the hall to the bathroom.

Somehow my recovery time was diminishing. At first I'd had fifteen "good" minutes. In the car on the way over, it had shrunk to about seven. Now there didn't seem to be any "good" minutes left. By now there *was* nothing left in me, but the urge continued. I lay on the floor outside the preschool room door, chin perched atop my butter tub, and prayed that God would take me right there. My only anchor to reality was the thought of Ethan, alone in the car.

The mom of a child I hardly knew bent over me. "Could I take Eva home with me after preschool for a while? Would that help you out?" she queried. I tried to bring her face into focus. *Did I even know this woman? What if she were a murderess or child abuser or mad rapist?* My mind was definitely gone. Why wouldn't the rest of me go too?

Gladly, I agreed and, with the motivation of her kindness, wrestled myself to my feet. Wobbling to the car, I repositioned my butter tub and drove home.

Once home, there was still Ethan. He was hungry and bored and his diaper stunk. I lay on the couch and clung to the phone, this time careful to keep it at my ear.

"Evan Morgan, please," I enunciated.

"Elisa?" LuAnne's clear voice came back to me. "Are you okay?" Dear, sweet, precious LuAnne. I told her I had the flu and desperately needed Evan to come home and help me. She told me he was still gone and wouldn't be back until mid-afternoon. I must have started crying, because then she announced, "Elisa, hang on. I'll right there."

The rest of the day is a blur. I remember LuAnne's blonde hair hovering over my feverish face, Ethan's giggles, the phone ringing, and soft voices humming. And blessed, restful, uninterrupted sleep.

Two are better than one.... If one falls down, his friend can help him up! the writer of Ecclesiastes preaches in chapter 4, verses 9 and 10. I knew these verses. I had read them often. But when had I put them into practice?

Why didn't I think of calling someone to help me that morning? I had called Evan, but not a friend. When I really needed a

companion along my flu journey, I'd reached for a rinsed-out butter tub.

Why? I picked up one excuse after another, examining their
offerings. *I don't want to bother anyone.* After all, other women had
their own children and schedules to keep. But to be honest, I knew
that wasn't the real reason. *I don't want to owe anyone.* How would I
ever repay their kindness? That was closer, but it still wasn't core.

Ah. Here it is. The real reason: *I'm not supposed to need anybody.
I'm supposed to do this myself and by myself. If I can't do this by myself,
there must be something wrong with me.*

Something was wrong with me, all right. I lacked a clear understanding of what was normal and what was abnormal. When the
Bible said, "Two are better than one," I figured, *But one who can do it
alone is even more mature.* And with such a definition of "maturity,"
I woke in the morning and went about my day, robbing myself of
the help in mothering I could have from others and from God.

Moms weren't designed to mother alone. By its very nature,
mothering is an "othering" process. We can't do it alone! So the flu
had proven to me.

No butter tub will ever look the same to me again. Written in
invisible letters lining the inside of all butter tubs everywhere is a
motto I've learned to take to heart: TWO ARE BETTER THAN ONE.

CONFIDENCE BUILDERS

1. Look back over your past week. How many times did you ask for and receive help from others?

2. Take a look at your view of receiving help. How do you view others who need help? How do you view yourself when you do things all alone? How do you believe others see you when you do ask for help?

3. What can you do to take advantage of the help with mothering that is available to you?

Two are better
than one.

Chapter ELEVEN

How Do I Show God to My Child?

The phone rang. It was Eva, calling from the school office. "Mom! You're going to kill me!" she blurted. "Mom! I'm sorry!" Visions of Eva wailing into the phone in front of three secretaries, the crosswalk guard, and maybe even the principal flashed through my mind. Kill her? Perhaps.

"Eva—tell me what's the matter!" I interrupted.

"Mom! I lost my retainer! You're going to kill me!" she responded.

She was right. I was going to kill her. Or was I? Eva is a very responsible child. *How should I respond to this? Was this a big deal?* I told her to meet me at the front office entrance, out of sight of the three secretaries, the crosswalk guard, and the principal.

On the way to the school a voice seemed to warn me. *Elisa, the way you respond to your daughter when she's nine and has lost her retainer is the way she will assume you'll respond to her when she is sixteen and has made a more serious mistake.* Hmmm. It's in these moments that I struggle with how to help my children understand God in the way I'm growing to understand him.

In the school parking lot, Eva poured out the whole story of leaving her retainer on the disposable lunch tray and then throwing the tray away. Being a mother, I'm willing to risk life and limb for the safe return of my child's retainer. After all, it cost one hundred fifty dollars. I scoured every lunchroom trash can and then interviewed the janitor, only to discover that the lunch trash had already been deposited in the outside dumpster. Shoulders set, jawline firm, I borrowed a lunchroom chair and began to hunt.

I hung from the waist over the side of the school's trash dumpster. For whole minutes at a time my feet left the wobbly cafeteria chair while my shirt stuck to the grunge on the metal edge. Scrunching up my nose in disgust, I gingerly picked through plastic sacks, which seemed to disintegrate at my touch. My central recollection is of peanut butter sandwiches soaked in chocolate milk. But no retainer.

By now Eva was crying again. She, too, had picked through more than a few soggy sandwiches and was more upset than ever at her predicament.

Like any other mother, I want my children to learn to be responsible: to make their beds in the morning, to brush their teeth without nagging, to do their homework, to fulfill commitments they make—like staying on the basketball team when they'd rather quit, or keeping a baby-sitting job even after receiving an invitation to a sleep over. I believe in the lessons of natural consequences—of living with broken toys that were used carelessly, of wearing dirty clothes that weren't put by the washing machine even after four pleas from me.

But I also believe in grace. *Charis,* the Greek word for grace, is one of the most difficult of all Greek words to translate into English. The application of this concept to life is even more challenging. I've spent most of my Christian life trying to understand and experience God's grace. My efforts have led me to the conclusion that we make God's grace much more complicated than he makes it.

Bottom line? When we're sorry, God forgives us and gives us another chance. First John 19 says, *If we confess our sins, he is faithful and just and will forgive us our sins and purify us from all unrighteousness.* Psalm 103:12 describes how far God's forgiveness goes: *As far as the east is from the west, so far has he removed our transgressions from us.*

That's what God does with my sins. Even in the moments when I'd responded too harshly to Eva's errors, God had forgiven me. She would somehow recover if I blew it again, but today I heard a warning. *How I respond today is how she will assume I'll respond in the future.* And more to the point—*What she finds in me is much of what she'll expect to find in God.* What our children need most in us is a model of what they have in Jesus.

She said she was sorry. And she meant it. Perhaps that was the key in this situation.

I got off the wobbly lunchroom chair, took Eva in my arms, and gave up the search. I told her that I forgave her. I called the orthodontist for an appointment and asked Eva for twenty-five dollars from her savings account to put toward the replacement. Then I let go of it. The way God lets go of all the mistakes I make.

Eva's been very careful with her new retainer, carrying it in a special case in her pocket whenever she eats. She brushes it faithfully and wears it day in and day out. So far, she still has it.

But last week she ate a Snickers bar two days after getting braces on her bottom teeth. And she broke a wire.

CONFIDENCE BUILDERS

1. How does the example of your parents impact your understanding of God?

2. How can you intentionally show God to your child?

The way we respond to our children's mistakes today is the way they'll assume we'll respond in the future. And what they find in us is much of what they expect to find in God.

Chapter TWELVE

How Do I Love My Child Enough But Not Too Much?

"How far is Missouri from Denver?" Eva asked.

My almost nine-year-old daughter was considering summer camp. She'd been squeamish about the Brownie overnighter in the first grade, but now, at her own initiative, she was interested in journeying across the country for two weeks to a camp she'd never seen.

In a way, I was delighted. After all, this spirit of independence and adventure was to be applauded. Hadn't I prayed for such a moment as this?

But how far was Missouri from Denver? I retreated to the basement to fetch the atlas—the *world atlas*! My child was considering going across the world! (Well, just across Kansas.) At nine years of age! And I wouldn't be there!

How could she manage if the hair in her sensitive scalp got tangled? What if they served hot dogs every night? She'd starve before she'd take one bite of a hot dog! What if she had a bad dream, couldn't make out my handwriting in my letters, or lost her toothbrush?

I couldn't help looking forward to a bit of a respite from responsibilities of mothering her for two weeks, but I also couldn't shake the haunting fears. What if she forgot about me and her brother and her dad for a while and was just herself? What if she grew up and away a bit more? What if she didn't need me in the same ways when she returned? What if she wasn't really ready and would be harmed by this separation? *Should I let her go? How was I supposed to love her enough but not too much?*

I've gone from an independent and free existence as an adult without children to the beck and call of a bundle weighing scarcely more than a well-stocked purse. And then, as soon as I adjust to losing my life to another, my little one decides she needs my help less than I want to give it. "I do it myself!" replaces her squawking insistence that I do it for her.

And so the cycle goes. *I need you. I want to do it by myself. I need you again. No, I don't.* How should I respond to this pendulum process? How do I figure out how much need is normal and how much is too much? How much love is love, and how much is suffocation?

Change is tough. When the Israelites returned from captivity in Babylon, they began rebuilding the temple by laying a new foundation on the site of the old structure.

And all the people gave a great shout to the LORD, because the foundation of the house of the LORD was laid. But many of the older priests and Levites and family heads, who had seen the former temple, wept aloud when they saw the foundation of this temple being laid, while many others shouted for joy. No one could distinguish the sound of the shouts of joy from the sound of weeping, because the people made so much noise. And the sound was heard far away.

(Ezra 3:11–13)

The old priests remembered the original temple in all its glory—the cedar paneling, the jeweled artwork. It stood centrally in their minds as *the* place where God dwelled. How could they see something different in its place—even if it was a new temple to house God?

The new priests exulted that *at last* the new was underway! The hands laying the stones were theirs. The voices raised in choruses were theirs. The old? Posh! God would dwell in the here and now of their lifetimes! Let's get on with it!

Oh, how I remember what was! Tiny fingers curled around mine, cheery cheeks smeared with graham crackers, toothless grins, sweaty hugs fresh from ball fields, tearful explanations. I remember the old temple.

How do we react to a little one's launching off our laps? To preschool? To the school bus and grade school? To junior high? To a driver's license? To college, an apartment of his or her own, a relationship, a marriage? To summer camp for two weeks in Missouri?

God has confidence in us. He holds us loosely so that we can grow. We must do the same with our children. We rejoice in what God has created. And grieve for what is no more.

I paused to ponder on the basement steps, wiped away the tears, fetched the world atlas and returned upstairs. I bought a footlocker, fourteen pairs of underwear, and went to the mailbox every day of those two weeks to look for a letter with a Missouri postmark.

CONFIDENCE BUILDERS

1. How do you feel about your child's growing more independent of you each day? What does your child's independence really say about you as a mother?

2. How can you apply God's loose grip on your life to how you can respond to your child?

3. When do you need to begin to let go of your child?

God has confidence in us. He holds us loosely so that we can grow. We must do the same with our children.

Chapter

THIRTEEN

How Can I Tell If I'm a Good Mom?

O ne of the most unsettling aspects of being a mom is that you never know just how you're doing at mothering. Most moms don't get a performance review until their children are in their late twenties or early thirties. Mother's Day bouquets are nice, though generally obligatory gestures purchased at the grocery store the night before. Birthdays and other holidays offer a smattering of warm memories whose messages seem to melt away once the event passes.

Some days, this not knowing doesn't bother me. I don't even have time to think about it. On a few occasions, however, I truly wonder, *How can I tell if I'm a good mom?* In such moments, my mind rewinds through its stored videos of memories and pauses on one in particular.

Eva and her dad had gone to run errands and planned to grab a bite to eat along the way. I hung up the phone from a long conversation to find Ethan looking at me with great expectation and asking, "What's for dinner?" Dinner? I wasn't even hungry. I'd wait for a large bowl of popcorn later on in the evening. But the clock read 6:05. Ethan had a point.

Usually I at least have a plan. Tacos from the leftover hamburger meat. A grilled cheese sandwich. Mac'n Cheese. But tonight I had a problem. This was a Sunday night. It doesn't matter if I go to the store on Tuesday, or Friday, or Saturday—by Sunday night there is no food in the house.

I opened the cupboard and peered inside while Ethan wormed in to look alongside me. Cheerios. An unopened bottle of ranch-style salad dressing. A jar of jelly. A package of jelly. A package of dried beans I'd bought during a season when I fancied myself a natural-food cook. That had been three years ago. As I surveyed the top of my nine-year-old's head, I decided that this was not the time to introduce Ethan to beans.

But wait—there in the back on the middle shelf—ah . . . Top Ramen. And—oooh . . . a can of chunk pineapple. Noodles for carbohydrates. The broth was made from some variety of meat. Fruit brought our total to three food groups. Good enough. Dinner.

Ethan approved the choice and busied himself with Legos while I took the ten minutes necessary to prepare the feast. I opened the can of pineapple and poured it into a serving bowl, its rich, fruity aroma wafting up at me. With my teeth, I ripped open the plastic pouch of dried noodles and watched them rehydrate in boiling water. When Ethan sat down to a vinyl placemat and paper napkin table setting, I served him a steaming bowl of Top Ramen with cheery pineapple chunks bordering the bowl on the plate below. A tall glass of cold milk sat in the spot where milk goes.

Perching beside him, I watched as he wrapped uncooperative noodles around his spoon and popped pineapple chunks into his mouth. We talked about school, sports, neighbors, and friends. Between bites and after a large swig of milk, Ethan looked at me with a serene smile and announced, "Mom, you're the best cook in the world! No—*you're the best mom in the world!*"

In an unexpected everyday moment of mothering, Top Ramen and chunk pineapple had christened me a good mom. *Is that all it takes?* I wanted to laugh! Top Ramen and pineapple chunks? There had been so many other times when I had tried *so* hard to be a good mom! *All* the hours spent making a costume only to discover that I'd sewn it together inside out! The *patience* I'd practiced with fingers as they twisted shoelaces into useless knots over and over again! The battles I'd fought over not wearing *those* shorts with *that* shirt, making beds, and getting homework done before TV. Not to mention the holiday-perfect meals I'd laid out on color-coordinated tables. To time the turkey to the vegetables and to unmold a Jello salad without its collapsing—these skills had taken me *years* to master! And now it all came down to Top Ramen and chunk pineapple! It seemed that even my outbursts of temper or periods of selfishness hadn't disqualified me from being a good mom. How simple it was, after all!

Ethan's pronouncement oozed into my heart and lodged there, its wisdom sinking into my soul. Perhaps it wasn't the food that so contented Ethan with me as a mom. Maybe it was my presence, perched beside him as he forked up the cubes of fruit and wrestled the wrinkled noodles into his mouth. There had been many moments, even that day, when my busyness had distanced and distracted me from his needs. Just an hour prior to "dinner," I'd cleaned out the cupboard below the kitchen sink, refilled the cat's litter box, and had been on the phone with my brother for about thirty minutes, all the while motioning Ethan away to his Legos, a cartoon show, or outside to play. The Top Ramen filled his tummy, but my attention, my focus on him and him alone, fed his soul.

There is another woman who, like me, struggled with getting "it" right in life. While the Bible doesn't specifically spell out what she was working at so hard, the general interpretation is that she was preparing a meal for guests who'd arrived to hear Jesus teach in her home. Martha stirred the pot and stoked the fire. She baked the bread and buttered the beans. She chopped the fruit and cheesed the potatoes. By herself. Shut away in the kitchen alone while her sister, Mary, sat at Jesus' feet and listened.

Luke 10:40 describes Martha as "distracted by all the preparations that had to be made." After all, there was a houseful of hungry people! They needed to eat! It was her job to feed them! And Mary should be helping her! Instead, Mary sat in Neverland, listening! Finally, fed up, she approached Jesus to reproach her sister.

And Jesus' response? In verse 41, he says, "Martha, Martha, you are worried and upset about many things, but only one thing is needed. Mary has chosen what is better . . . ." While Martha had been fretting about feeding her guests, they, along with Mary, had been feasting on the food of Jesus' teaching. Martha—empty and hungry herself—had frenzied to feed others. Mary—aware of her great need for God and that her need was like that of her guests—relaxed in Jesus' presence—aware that together she and her guests were dining on the true food needed by their souls.

Only one thing is needed. Top Ramen and chunk pineapple are an adequate supper for a boy who is more interested in dining on his mother's presence.

How can I tell if I'm a good mom? Well, I work at being more a Mary and less a Martha. I, myself, dine on the presence of Jesus so that my children can find what they need in me. I focus less on a color-coordinated table setting and more on making sure that I serve up enough of me. And I listen in the every day for the assessments of my efforts in the words of a little boy who thinks a feast of Top Ramen and pineapple chunks makes me the best cook—no, the best *mom*—in the world.

CONFIDENCE BUILDERS

1. When you think about qualities that make up a "good mom," what characteristics top your list? According to your list, how are you doing?

2. How does the story of Mary and Martha change your view of what makes a "good mom"?

3. Are there ways you could grow to be more like Mary and less like Martha? What distracts you from feeding your soul on Jesus' words?

Being a good mom isn't complicated. Only one thing is needed. When we, ourselves, dine on the presence of Jesus, our children will find in us what they need.

Afterword

In 1962 my mother made it through a difficult day with a nine-year-old, a seven-year-old, and an eighteen-month-old. It was difficult because she was in a new home in a state far away from her own family and friends. It was difficult because she was working full-time while trying to raise us. And it was difficult because she was doing this all alone. She was divorced.

At the time, I didn't appreciate her struggle. Even ten years ago, newly awed with my own toddler, I didn't grasp the fact that she'd actually experienced much of what I was facing. But now, looking back over my life and hers, I've come to understand that while she may not have parented me perfectly, she did, indeed, share some of the questions, the inadequacies, and the small victories that litter my daily path.

A few years ago, just after my mother died, my brother dug through boxes and unearthed her writings. Poems. Short stories. Essays. Words put to paper that her friends and children had never seen before. Sentences that made sense of what we had wondered about her life. As a memorable memento of my mother, my brother presented to me and my sister a copy of a thin, personal, self-published book.

I still remember the moment I opened this gift—touching the black sturdy cover, opening the book to discover her portrait, turning page after page to take in her words. Near the end of the book, one entry caused me to pause and ponder. Indeed, every mother asks the question in her heart. Even my own.

Whether it's 1962 or now, my mother or me, your mother or you, moms all struggle with whether or not they have what it takes to mother and to mother well. When we verbalize our wonderings, we find strength, courage, and yes, even confidence in ourselves as mothers.

Where Is Noon?

by Paige Lee, 1962

Saturday morning is Mommy's Time at our house. This got started because I love to sleep. Five of the other days are school days with the normal early morning bedlam. The remaining day is for Sunday school, which starts at 9:00 A.M. in our church.

Mommy's Time means that on Saturday mornings, Cathy, who is nine, gets our toddler up, gives him his breakfast, and puts him back to bed for his morning nap while Elisa, who is seven, fixes cereal and sweet rolls. This means I can sleep, oh, sometimes clear up until 9:00 A.M., if the splash of milk or the spilling of cereal or the sounds of bickering don't force me up sooner. Some Saturdays it's a benighted favor, but sometimes there is a delicious silence, and I burrow deeper into the covers and know the lovely luxury of waking up leisurely.

Today is Saturday, but it sure isn't Mommy's Time. My Saturday started somewhere around 5:30 A.M., when I was startled awake by the howling and frantic wind swirling around our house so strongly that I was reminded of the three little pigs and the wolf and wondered if the huffing and puffing would blow our small cottage away! The rain was a machine gun at my windows, and a hiss in the drainpipes, a snake slithering in under the garage doors. I put on a robe and went around peering out windows. The radio, which I had flipped on in passing, told me in the cheery early morning tones of a disk jockey that the storm was only the beginning.

And he was so right.

Actually, it was a fairly normal Saturday morning. Thank the Lord for TV cartoons in wintertime! By 8:00 A.M. I felt sure that it must be noon. The children were excited with the wildness of the storm for, in their years and in our part of California, they had never seen one before. Cathy had brought the milk in, dropping the half-gallon bottle, which made a storm of its own, with the splinters of glass flying everywhere. We put the baby back in his crib while I cleaned up the mess. At this point he evidently decided that it was time for potty training, as he removed all of his clothes and baptized half the room before being discovered. Breakfast was louder than usual, with the children's excitement making voices louder, tempers shorter. Elisa turned over the sugar bowl, and the baby put cereal in every conceivable place except his mouth.

By 10:00 A.M., eight soggy friends of theirs of varying ages and sexes had dripped their way into the den to watch cartoons on TV. Three or more had, for some odd reason, actually removed their storm gear in the kitchen, and all eleven, plus my two, had said, "Gee, I'm hungry," at least twice. I later bundled up the girls to take them to a birthday party, making the baby only an hour late for his nap ('cause, of course, he had to go too) and, between taking them and picking them up (and getting the baby down), I was able to make several of the Girl Scout calls I had pending. Before the girls were well into the car, they remembered the dresses they'd each received from their father's mother the day before and were beseeching me to have them pressed before church time tomorrow. To the music of this plea, I fought my way home through the storm.

It's now 5:00 P.M., I've mopped the floor at least three times, doled out apples, chauffeured to Timbuktu and back, settled four fights, changed several diapers, answered the telephone about twenty times, and wondered at least fifty times: *Who ever invented children and motherhood, anyway?* I'm beginning to get the sniffles, the rain is still pelting, the wind is still howling, dinner is still ahead of me, and my lips are compressed and hurting to keep me from throwing something and saying, *Forget the whole thing.*

I hate everyone.

It's now 7:00 P.M. I've just fed the baby and gotten him down, and put a load of diapers in the wash. The girls are eating, and I have just finished pressing their two new dresses. Elisa hugs me, and Cathy says, "Mommy, I hope, when I grow up, I can be as good and wonderful a mommy as you."

The rain is still machine-gunning my windows, and the huff-and-puff of the wolf wind is still with me. My house suddenly feels cozy. I think I'll build a fire, and perhaps the girls can roast marshmallows tonight.

The MOPS Story

From its humble beginnings in a church in Wheat Ridge, Colorado, in 1973, MOPS International now charters MOPS groups in about two thousand churches in the United States and several other countries.

Some seventy thousand moms are touched by their local MOPS group, and many, many more are encouraged through the media arms of MOPS: *Mom Sense* radio and newsletter, and publications such as this book. MOPS groups meet the unique needs of mothers of preschoolers in a variety of settings, including urban, suburban, rural, and Teen MOPS. Mission MOPS provides funds for organizations that need financial assistance for MOPS group leadership training and chartering.

MOPS grew out of a desire to meet the nine needs of every mother of preschoolers. Today, when a mom enters a MOPS meeting, she is greeted by a friendly face and escorted to the MOPPETS program, where her children enjoy their special part of the MOPS program. In MOPPETS, children from infancy through kindergarten experience a caring environment while being introduced to crafts, songs, and learning opportunities.

Once her children are settled, the MOPS mom joins a program tailor-made to meet her needs. She can grab something good to eat and not have to share it! She can finish a sentence and not have to speak in Children-ese!

The program begins with a brief lesson taught by an older mom who's been through the challenging early years of mothering and who can share from her experience and from the truths taught in the Bible. Then the women move into small discussion groups where each mom is free to share her joys and struggles with other moms who truly understand her feelings.

From here, the women participate in a craft activity. For moms who are often frustrated by the impossibility of completing anything in their unpredictable days, this activity is deeply satisfying. It provides a sense of accomplishment and growth for many moms.

Because moms of preschoolers themselves lead MOPS, the program also offers women a chance to develop their leadership skills and other talents. It takes organization, financial management, creativity, and management skills to run a MOPS program successfully.

By the time they finish the MOPS meeting and pick up their children, the moms feel refreshed and better able to mother. MOPS helps them recognize that moms have needs too! And when they take the time to meet those needs, they find they are more effective in meeting the needs of their families.

If you're interested in finding out general information about MOPS please write the MOPS International office:

MOPS International
PO Box 102200
Denver, CO 80250–2200

To find out if there is a MOPS group in your area call 303–733–5353 or 1–800–929–1287. Fax: 303–733–5770.
To start a MOPS group, please call 888–910–MOPS.

E-mail: Info@MOPS.org
Web Site:http://www.MOPS.org